The Sayings of Moses

THE SAYINGS OF THE GREAT RELIGIOUS LEADERS

Editor: Andrew Linzey

The Sayings of Jesus

Selected by Andrew Linzey
Director of the Centre for the Study of Theology in the
University of Essex

The Sayings of Moses

Selected by Dan Cohn-Sherbok
University Lecturer in Jewish Theology in the
University of Kent

The Sayings of Muhammad

Selected and Translated by Neal Robinson
Senior Lecturer in Religious Studies in the Cheltenham
and Gloucester College of Higher Education

The Sayings of the Buddha

Selected by Geoffrey Parrinder
Emeritus Professor of Comparative Study of Religions in
the University of London, King's College

The Sayings of

MOSES

selected by

DAN COHN-SHERBOK

DUCKWORTH

First published in 1991 by
Gerald Duckworth & Co. Ltd.
The Old Piano Factory
43 Gloucester Crescent, London NW1 7DY

All biblical quotations are taken from
The Torah: The Five Books of Moses
(Jewish Publication Society,
Philadelphia, © 1967). All rabbinic
quotations are taken from C.G. Montefiore
& H. Loewe, *A Rabbinic Anthology*
(Schocken, New York, © 1974).

ISBN 0 7156 2375 3

British Library Cataloguing in Publication Data
The Sayings of Moses.
   1. Judaism
   I. Cohn-Sherbok, Dan
296

   ISBN 0-7156-2375-3

Photoset in North Wales by
Derek Doyle & Associates, Mold, Clwyd
Printed in Great Britain by
Redwood Press Limited, Melksham

Introduction

In the Hebrew scriptures Moses is presented as the
leader of his people and the supreme lawgiver, and his
presence dominates the Five Books of Moses. Born in
Egypt, he was the son of Amram and Jochebed. At the
time of his birth Pharaoh had declared that all first-born
males of the Hebrew nation should be killed. At first
Moses was hidden in his parents' home, but in
desperation Jochebed deposited him in a wicker basket
on the Nile, where he was discovered by Pharaoh's
daughter. He grew up in the royal household. One day
he saw an Egyptian taskmaster abuse a Hebrew slave. In
anger he killed the Egyptian and fled from Egypt to
Midian, where he married Zipporah, the daughter of
Jethro the priest. While he was tending his father-in-
law's sheep, God appeared to him in the midst of a
burning bush and instructed him to return to Egypt to
free the Israelites from bondage. He was reluctant to
accept this mission, but eventually complied and
appeared before Pharaoh pleading for his people.

God afflicted the Eygptians with ten plagues, and
Pharaoh was persuaded to release the Israelites. But he
later changed his mind and the Egyptians set out in
pursuit. When they arrived at the Red Sea, Moses raised
his staff, the sea parted and the Israelites crossed on dry
land. Pharaoh's hosts, however, were drowned in the
sea as the waters closed over them. Moses and all the
people sang a song of praise to God.

After wandering in the desert the Israelites came to
Mount Sinai. Moses ascended the mountain, where he
remained for forty days and nights and received the
Tablets of the Law. But during his absence the people
made a golden calf to worship. Eventually he descended
from Mount Sinai, observed their idolatry, smashed the
Tablets, burned the calf, ground the gold to powder,
scattered it on the water and made the Israelites drink it.
He then went up a second time, and returned with

another set of Tablets and the entire legal code contained in the Pentateuch ('five books').

In his subsequent sojourn in the desert, instead of speaking to a rock as God had commanded Moses struck it to obtain water. As a punishment, he was prevented from entering the Promised Land. When the Israelites reached its boundary, he gathered the people, delivered a final address containing a summary of the Sinaitic legislation and ascended Mount Nebo to die.

According to tradition, Moses was the greatest of all the prophets in the history of the nation: 'Never again did there arise in Israel a prophet like Moses – whom the Lord singled out, face to face, for the various signs and portents that the Lord sent him to display in the land of Egypt, against Pharaoh and all his courtiers and his whole country, and for all the great might and awesome power that Moses displayed before all Israel' (Deuteronomy 34:10-12).

Traditional Judaism maintains that the Five Books of Moses were dictated by God to Moses. This doctrine implies that the entire text – including all the sayings of Moses – are ultimately of divine origin. Such a belief guarantees the validity of the account of Moses' call, the Exodus, the revelation on Mount Sinai, the legal system and the granting of the Promised Land. In the modern period, however, it has become increasingly difficult to sustain this concept of Scripture. As early as the sixteenth century scholars pointed out that the Five Books of Moses appear to be composed of different sources. In the nineteenth century sustained investigation by two German scholars, Karl Heinrich Graf and Julius Wellhausen, concluded that they were composed of four main documents which once existed separately but were later combined by a series of editors or redactors. The first document (J), dating from the ninth century BC, attributes an anthropomorphic character to God, who is referred to by the four Hebrew letters YHWH. The second source (E), stemming from the eighth century, is less anthropomorphic and uses the divine name 'Elohim'. The third (D), from the seventh century, concentrates on religious purity and the priesthood. Finally, the P source, from the fifth century, which has a more transcendental view of God, emphasises the importance of the sacrificial cult.

Using this framework, Graf and Wellhausen maintained that it is was possible to account for the manifold problems and discrepancies in the Biblical text. This hypothesis was modified by subsequent writers. Some scholars have preferred not to speak of separate sources, but of circles of tradition; on this view J, E, P and D represent oral traditions rather than written documents. Further, they stress that the separate traditions themselves contain early material; thus it is a mistake to think that they originated in their entirety at particular periods. Others reject the theory of separate sources altogether, arguing that oral traditions were modified throughout the history of ancient Israel and were only gradually compiled into a single narrative. Yet despite these different theories there is a general recognition among scholars that the Five Books of Moses were not written by Moses; they are seen rather as a collection of traditions originating at different times in ancient Israel. The historical reliability of Moses' utterances in the Pentateuch has thus been called into question. It may well be that the majestic sayings of Moses were written at a later time and anachronistically attributed to him as the leader of the nation.

Textual studies of ancient manuscripts also highlight the improbability of the Jewish view of Scripture. According to tradition, the Hebrew text of the Five Books used in synagogues today is the same as that given to Moses. Yet it is widely accepted among scholars that the script of contemporary Torah scrolls is different from the script current in ancient Israel from the time of the monarchy until the sixth century BC. Furthermore, the fact that ancient translations of the Hebrew Bible into languages such as Syriac and Greek contain variant readings suggests that the Hebrew text of the Pentateuch now in use is not entirely free from error.

Finally, there is the influence of the ancient Near East on the Bible. Archaeology has shown that there are strong parallels in the Bible to laws, stories and myths found throughout the ancient Near East. It is unlikely that this is simply a coincidence. The authors of the Biblical period shared much the same world view as their neighbours and no doubt transformed this framework to fit their own religious notions. Most scholars would find it impossible to reconcile the traditional conceptions of Mosaic authorship of the Five Books with the findings of modern Biblical scholarship and scientific discovery.

As for the narrative of the Exodus, here also the details are very uncertain. Some scholars have suggested that the crossing of the Red Sea took place not at the head of the Gulf of Suez, which is a long way from the Israelites' point of departure, but at one of the lakes now joined by the Suez Canal or at the head of the Gulf of Aqaba, or at Lake Sirbonis. The mountain where God revealed Himself to Moses has traditionally been identified with Jebel Musa in the south of Sinai, but such a location would have taken the Israelites dangerously near the route the Egyptans used to reach copper and turquoise mines in that area. Another suggestion is that the occurrences on the mountain signify volcanic activity: since no mountain in the Sinai peninsula is volcanic, it has been advanced that the site was in north-western Arabia, east of the Gulf of Aqaba.

The Bible therefore does not enable us to trace the route of the Jews in the wilderness. Questions have also been raised about the date. I Kings 6:1 says that the Exodus took place 480 years before Solomon founded the Temple (in the fourth year of his reign). Assuming that he came to the throne in 961 BC this would have been in 1438. But if the Israelites laboured at Pithom and Raamses as Scripture relates, it would have been much later. So from a historical viewpoint, the Exodus, like the Biblical account of Moses himself, poses a number of serious difficulties.

Despite these uncertainties about the historical accuracy of Scripture, Moses remains the central figure of the Torah. Yet in the Bible he is presented as a human person possessing faults and frailties: when he saw an Egyptian beating a Hebrew slave, he was overcome with rage and killed him. Called by God to lead the Israelites from Egypt, he felt inadequate to the task. Unsure of his abilities, he doubted that the Israelites would listen to him because he had a speech impediment. At Mount Sinai he shattered the Tablets of the Law when he saw the people worshipping a golden calf. Later he was barred from entering the Promised Land because he had struck a rock in anger. Moses is thus not conceived as a divine or semi-divine figure. Unlike Christianity, which elevates Jesus as Redeemer and Saviour, the Jewish faith affirms that no person – not even Moses – should be regarded as the focus of the religion. It is God – not Moses – who gave the Torah to the nation; it is He who watches over his chosen people and guides them to their ultimate destiny. Only in this context can Moses' role in Jewish history be understood.

Thus for the Jews Moses is 'Moshe Rabbenu' ('Moses, our Master'), the teacher of the Torah. As the greatest Biblical figure, he is the servant of God, the Lawgiver, Liberator, and moulder of the Jewish people. In rabbinic sources, as illustrated by the rabbinic sayings collected at the end of this book, he is described as the profound believer, the greatest of the prophets, and the faithful leader. The principles of love and justice which he laid down serve as the foundation of the Jewish faith. Three thousand years after his death the religion he founded endures, and his abiding trust in God has inspired generations. His quest for liberation and righteousness has echoed down the ages and he remains a symbol of dedication and freedom. Today as Jews stand on the threshold of the twenty-first century Moses' words remain as significant as they were in ancient times when he gathered the people together before Mount Sinai and called them to the worship of the One true God, the creator of Heaven and Earth.

The Call

According to Scripture, Moses was born at the height of
the Egyptian persecution of the Hebrews. Concealed
among the Nile reeds, he was rescued by Pharaoh's
daughter and brought up in the royal palace. Although
raised as an Egyptian, he was drawn to his kinspeople.
When he saw an Egyptian taskmaster beat a Hebrew
slave, he killed the Egyptian. Out of fear of discovery, he
fled to Midian where he was a shepherd of his
father-in-law Jethro. There God appeared to him out of a
burning bush, and charged him with a divine mission to
rescue the Hebrews from bondage. At first he tried to
resist the call, but finally he accepted God's decree.

*

I must turn aside to look at this marvellous sight; why
doesn't the bush burn up?

Exodus 3:3

Here am I.

Exodus 3:4

Please, O Lord, make someone else Your agent.

Exodus 4:13

Please, O Lord, I have never been a man of words, either
in times past or now that You have spoken to Your
servant; I am slow of speech and slow of tongue.

Exodus 4:10

Who am I that I should go to Pharaoh and free the
Israelites from Egypt?

Exodus 3:11

When I come to the Israelites and say to them 'The God
of your fathers has sent me to you', and they ask me,
'What is His name?' what shall I say to them?

Exodus 3:13

What if they do not believe me and do not listen to
me, but say: 'The Lord did not appear to you?'

Exodus 4:1

See, You say to me, 'Lead this people forward', but You
have not made known to me whom You will send with
me. Further, You have said, 'I have singled you out by
name, and you have, indeed, gained My favour.' Now if
I have truly gained Your favour, pray let me know Your
ways that I may know You and continue in Your favour.

Exodus 33:12-13

The Israelites would not listen to me; how then should
Pharaoh heed me, a man of impeded speech!

Exodus 6:12

O Lord, why did You bring harm upon this people?
Why did you send me? Ever since I came to Pharaoh to
speak in Your name, he has dealt worse with this
people; and still You have not delivered Your people.

Exodus 5:22-23

Oh, let me behold Your Presence!

Exodus 33:18

Exodus

Moses led the departure from Egypt. With his brother Aaron he appeared before Pharaoh and declared: 'Let my people go!' God sent one plague after another to persuade Pharaoh to release the Hebrews. The last plague – the death of the Egyptian first-born – succeeded. Yet after they departed, Pharaoh sought to recapture them. When they reached the Red Sea, they crossed on dry land while the pursuing Egyptians were drowned. In celebration of their deliverance, they sang a song of triumph with Moses.

*

Let my people go.   Exodus 5:1

The Lord, the God of the Hebrews, sent me to you to say, 'Let My people go that they may worship Me in the wilderness.' But you have paid no heed until now. Thus says the Lord, 'By this shall you know that I am the Lord.' See, I shall strike the water in the Nile with the rod that is in my hand, and it will be turned into blood; and the fish in the Nile will die. The Nile will stink so that the Egyptians will find it impossible to drink the water of the Nile.'

Exodus 7:16-18

Thus says the Lord: 'Let My people go that they may worship Me. If you refuse to let them go, then I will plague your whole country with frogs. The Nile shall swarm with frogs, and they shall come up and enter your palace, your bedchamber and your bed, the houses of your courtiers and your people, and your ovens and your kneading bowls.'

Exodus 7:26-28

Thus says the Lord, 'Let My people go that they may worship Me. For if you do not let My people go, I will let loose swarms of insects against you and your courtiers and your people and your houses; the houses of the Egyptians, and the very ground they stand on, shall be filled with swarms of insects.'

Exodus 8:16-17

Thus says the Lord, the God of the Hebrews, 'Let My people go to worship Me. For if you refuse to let them go, and continue to hold them, then the hand of the Lord will strike your livestock in the fields – the horses, the asses, the camels, the cattle, and the sheep – with a very severe pestilence.'

Exodus 9:1-3

Thus says the Lord, the God of the Hebrews, 'Let My people go to worship Me. For this time I will send all My plagues upon your person, and your courtiers, and your people, in order that you may know that there is none like Me in all the world … This time tomorrow I will rain down a very heavy hail, such as has not been in Egypt from the day it was founded until now. Therefore, order your livestock and everything you have in the open brought under shelter; every man and beast that is found outside, not having been brought indoors, shall perish when the hail comes down upon them!'

Exodus 9:13-14, 18-19

Thus says the Lord, the God of the Hebrews, 'How long will you refuse to humble yourself before Me? Let My people go that they may worship Me. For if you refuse to let My people go, tomorrow I will bring locusts on your territory. They shall cover the surface of the land, so that no one will be able to see the land. They shall devour the surviving remnant that was left to you after the hail; and they shall eat away all your trees that grow in the field. Moreover, they shall fill your palaces and the houses of all your courtiers and of all the Egyptians – something that neither your fathers nor your fathers' fathers have seen from the day they appeared on earth to this day.'

Exodus 10:3-6

Thus says the Lord, 'Towards midnight I will go forth among the Egyptians, and every first-born in the land of Egypt shall die, from the first-born of Pharaoh who sits on his throne to the first-born of the slave girl who is behind the millstones; and all the first-born of the cattle. And there shall be a loud cry in all the land of Egypt, such as has never been or will ever be again; but not a dog shall snarl at any of the Israelites at man or beast – in order that you may know that the Lord makes a distinction between Egypt and Israel.'

Exodus 11:4-7

Take a bunch of hyssop, dip it in the blood that is in the basin, and apply some of the blood that is in the basin to the lintel and to the two doorposts. None of you shall go outside the door of his house until morning. For when the Lord goes through to smite the Egyptians, He will see the blood on the lintel and the two doorposts, and the Lord will pass over the door and not let the Destroyer enter and smite your home.

Exodus 12:22-23

Thus says the Lord, 'Israel is My first-born son. I have said to you, ''Let My son go, that he may worship Me'', yet you refuse to let him go. Now I will slay your first-born son.'

Exodus 3:22-23

I will sing to the Lord for He has triumphed gloriously. Horse and driver He has hurled into the sea.

Exodus 15:1

The Lord, the Warrior – Lord is His name! Pharaoh's chariots and his army He has cast into the sea; and the pick of his officers are drowned in the Sea of Reeds. The deeps covered them; they went down into the depths like a stone.

Exodus 15:3-5

In Your great triumph You break Your opponents; You
send forth Your fury, it consumes them like straw. At
the blast of Your nostrils the waters piled up, the floods
stood straight like a wall. The deeps froze in the heart of
the sea.

Exodus 15:7-8

You have seen all that the Lord did before your very
eyes in the land of Egypt to Pharaoh and to all his
courtiers and to his whole country: the wondrous feats
that you saw with your own eyes, those prodigious
signs and marvels. Yet to this day the Lord has not
given you a mind to understand or eyes to see, or ears to
hear.

Deuteronomy 29:1-3

You have seen what I did to the Egyptians, how I bore
you on eagles' wings.

Exodus 19:4

Why do you quarrel with me? Why do you try the Lord?

Exodus 17:2

Remember this day, on which you went free from
Egypt, the house of bondage, how the Lord freed you
from it with a mighty hand; no leavened bread shall be
eaten ... seven days you shall eat unleavened bread.

Exodus 13:3,6

I cannot bear the burden of you by myself ... How can I
bear unaided the trouble of you, and the burden, and
the bickering!

Deuteronomy 1:9,12

What shall I do with this people? Before long they will
be stoning me!

Exodus 17:4

Remember, never forget, how you provoked the Lord
your God to anger in the wilderness: from the day that
you left the land of Egypt until you reached this place,
you have continued defiant toward the Lord.

Deuteronomy 9:7

Remember the long way that the Lord your God has made you travel in the wilderness these past forty years, that He might test you by hardships to learn what was in your hearts; whether you would keep His commandments or not. He subjected you to the hardship of hunger and then gave you manna to eat, which neither you nor your fathers had ever known, in order to teach you that man does not live on bread alone.

Deuteronomy 8:2-3

When, in time to come, your son asks you, 'What mean the exhortations, laws and rules which the Lord our God has enjoined upon you?' you shall say to your son, 'We were slaves to Pharaoh in Egypt and the Lord freed us from Egypt with a mighty hand.'

Deuteronomy 6:20-21

You too must befriend the stranger, for you were strangers in the land of Egypt.

Deuteronomy 10:19

Your ancestors went down to Egypt seventy persons in all; and now the Lord your God has made you as numerous as the stars of heaven.

Deuteronomy 10:22

The Lord wrought before our eyes marvellous and destructive signs and wonders in Egypt, against Pharaoh and all his household; and us He freed from these, that He might take us and give us the land that He promised on oath to our fathers.

Deuteronomy 6:22-23

Has any god ventured to go and take himself one nation from the midst of another by prodigious acts, by signs and portents, by war, by a mighty and an outstretched arm and awesome power, as the Lord your God did for you in Egypt before your very eyes?

Deuteronomy 4:34

Revelation

After a period of wandering in the desert, the Hebrews reached Mount Sinai. There God appeared to them and through Moses gave them the Ten Commandments. Moses went up the mountain, where he remained for forty days and forty nights to receive the Tablets of the Covenant. While he was on the top of the mountain, the people made a golden calf to serve as their god. When Moses returned he broke the Tablets in anger, burnt the calf, ground the gold to dust and scattered it on the water, which he made the Hebrews drink. He then ascended Mount Sinai again and returned with a second set of Tablets containing God's law.

*

The Lord spoke those words – those and no more – to your whole congregation at the mountain, with a mighty voice out of the fire, and the dense clouds. He inscribed them on two tablets of stone, which He gave to me.

Deuteronomy 5:19

From the heavens He let you hear His voice to discipline you; on earth He let you see His great fire; and from amidst that fire you heard His words.

Deuteronomy 4:36

You have but to inquire about bygone ages that came before you, ever since God created man on earth, from one end of heaven to the other: has anything as grand as this ever happened, or has its like ever been known. Has any people heard the voice of a god speaking out of a fi   as you have, and survived?

Deuteronomy 4:32-33

Take utmost care and watch yourselves scrupulously, so that you do not forget the things that you saw with your own eyes and so that they do not fade from your mind as long as you live. And make them known to your children and to your children's children.

Deuteronomy 4:9

Face to face the Lord spoke to you on the mountain out of the fire – I stood between the Lord and you at that time to convey the Lord's words to you.

Deuteronomy 5:4-5

You came forward and stood at the foot of the mountain. The mountain was ablaze with flames to the very skies, dark with densest clouds. The Lord spoke to you out of the fire; you heard the sound of words but perceived no shape – nothing but a voice.

Deuteronomy 4:11-12

For your own sake, therefore, be most careful – since you saw no shape when the Lord your God spoke to you at Horeb out of the fire – not to act wickedly and make for yourselves a sculptured image in any likeness whatever: the form of a man or a woman, the form of any beast on earth, the form of any winged bird that flies in the sky, the form of anything that creeps on the ground, the form of any fish that is in the waters below the earth. And when you look up to the sky and behold the sun and the moon and the stars, the whole heavenly host, you must not be lured into bowing down to them or serving them.

Deuteronomy 4:15-19

The Lord spoke those words – those and no more – to your whole congregation at the mountain, with a mighty voice out of the fire and the dense clouds. He inscribed them on two tablets of stone, which He gave to me. When you heard the voice out of the darkness, while the mountain was ablaze with fire, you came up to me, all your tribal heads and elders, and said, 'The Lord our God has just shown us His majestic Presence, and we have heard His voice out of the fire; we have seen this day that man may live though God has spoken to him. Let us not die, then, for this fearsome fire will consume us; if we hear the voice of the Lord our God any longer, we shall die.'

Deuteronomy 5:19-22

I had ascended the mountain to receive the tablets of stone, the Tablets of the Covenant that the Lord had made with you, and I stayed on the mountain forty days and forty nights, eating no bread and drinking no water. And the Lord gave me the two tablets of stone inscribed by the finger of God, with the exact words that the Lord had addressed to you out of the fire on the day of the Assembly.

Deuteronomy 9:9-10

At the end of those forty days and forty nights, the Lord gave me the two tablets of stone, the Tablets of the Covenant. And the Lord said to me, 'Hurry, go down from here at once, for the people whom you brought out of Egypt have acted wickedly; they have been quick to stray from the path that I enjoined upon them; they have made themselves a molten image.'

Deuteronomy 9:11-12

I started down the mountain, a mountain ablaze with fire, the two Tablets of the Covenant in my two hands. I saw how you had sinned against the Lord your God; you had made yourselves a molten calf; you had been quick to stray from the path that the Lord had enjoined upon you. Thereupon I gripped the two tablets and flung them away with both my hands, smashing them before your eyes.

Deuteronomy 9:15-17

As for that sinful thing you had made, the calf, I took it and put it to the fire; I broke it to bits and ground it thoroughly until it was as fine as dust, and I threw its dust into the brook that comes down from the mountain.

Deuteronomy 9:21

When I lay prostrate before the Lord those forty days and forty nights, because the Lord was determined to destroy you, I prayed to the Lord and said, 'O Lord God, do not annihilate Your very own people, whom You redeemed in Your majesty and whom You freed from Egypt with a mighty hand. Give thought to Your servants, Abraham, Isaac, and Jacob, and pay no heed to the stubbornness of this people, its wickedness, and its sinfulness.

Deuteronomy 9:25-27

I took the two tablets with me and went up the mountain. The Lord inscribed on the tablets the same text as on the first, the Ten Commandments that He addressed to you on the mountain out of the fire on the day of the Assembly; and the Lord gave them to me. Then I left and went down from the mountain.

Deuteronomy 10:3-5

Thereupon the Lord said to me, 'Carve out two tablets of stone like the first, and come up to Me on the mountain; and make an ark of wood. I will inscribe on the tablets the commandments that were on the first tablets which you smashed, and you shall deposit them in the ark.'

Deuteronomy 19:1-2

And now, O Israel, what does the Lord your God demand of you? Only this: to revere the Lord your God, to walk only in His paths, to love Him, and to serve the Lord your God with all your heart and soul.

Deuteronomy 10:12

And now, O Israel, give heed to the laws and rules which I am instructing you to observe, so that you may live to enter and occupy the land the Lord, the God of your fathers, is giving you. You shall not add anything to what I command you or take anything away from it.

Deuteronomy 4:1-2

You shall love the Lord your God with all your heart
and with all your soul and with all your might. Take to
heart these instructions with which I charge you this
day. Impress them upon your children. Recite them
when you stay at home and when you are away, when
you lie down and when you get up. Bind them as a sign
on your hand and let them serve as symbol on your
forehead; inscribe them on the doorposts of your house
and on your gates.

Deuteronomy 6:5-9

You have been guilty of a great sin. Yet I will go up to
the Lord; perhaps I may win forgiveness for your sin.

Exodus 32:30

If I have gained Your favour, O Lord, pray, let the Lord
go in our midst, even though this is a stiffnecked
people. Pardon our iniquity and our sin, and take us for
Your own!

Exodus 34:8-9

If, then, you obey the commandments that I enjoin
upon you this day, loving the Lord your God and
serving Him with all your heart and soul, I will grant the
rain for your land in season, the early rain and the late.

Deuteronomy 11:13

See, this day I set before you blessing and curse.

Deuteronomy 11:26

You stand this day, all of you, before the Lord your God
– your tribal heads, your elders and your officials, all the
men of Israel, your children, your wives, even the
stranger within your camp, from woodchopper to
waterdrawer – to enter into the covenant of the Lord
your God.

Deuteronomy 29:9-11

You shall faithfully observe all My laws and all My
regulations, lest the land to which I bring you to settle in
spew you out.

Leviticus 20:22

If you do not obey the Lord your God to observe
faithfully all His commandments and laws which I
enjoin upon you this day, all these curses shall come
upon you and take effect: Cursed shall you be in the city
and cursed shall you be in the country. Cursed shall be
your basket and your kneading bowl. Cursed shall be
the issue of your womb and the produce of your soil, the
calving of your herd and the lambing of your flock.
Cursed shall you be in your comings and cursed shall
you be in your goings.

Deuteronomy 28:15-19

Choose life – if you and your offspring would live – by
loving the Lord your God, heeding His commands, and
holding fast to Him.

Deuteronomy 30:19-20

See, I set before you this day life and prosperity, death
and adversity.

Deuteronomy 30:15

If you fail to observe faithfully all the terms of this
teaching that are written in this book, to reverence this
honoured and awesome Name, the Lord your God will
inflict extraordinary plagues upon you and your
offspring, strange and lasting plagues, malignant and
chronic diseases. He will bring back upon you all the
sicknesses of Egypt that you dreaded so.

Deuteronomy 28:58-60

If you do not obey the Lord your God ... the Lord will let
loose against you calamity, panic and frustration ... the
Lord will strike you with madness, blindness, and
dismay. You shall grope at noon as a blind man gropes
in the dark.

Deuteronomy 28:15,20,28

The Lord will make you the head, not the tail; you will
always be at the top and never at the bottom – if only
you obey and faithfully observe the commandments of
the Lord your God.

Deuteronomy 28:13

You have affirmed this day that the Lord is your God, that you will walk in His ways, that you will observe His laws and commandments and rules, and that you will obey Him. And the Lord has affirmed this day that you are, as He promised you, His treasured people – and that He will set you, in fame and renown and glory, high above all the nations that He has made.

> Deuteronomy 26:17-19

The Lord your God will raise up for you a prophet from among your own people, like myself; him you shall heed.

> Deuteronomy 18:15

Any prophet who presumes to speak in My name an oracle which I did not command him to utter, or who speaks in the name of other gods – that prophet shall die.

> Deuteronomy 18:20

You shall not act at all as we now act here, every man as he pleases.

> Deuteronomy 12:8

Silence! Hear, O Israel! today you have become the people of the Lord your God: heed the Lord your God and observe His commandments and His laws.

> Deuteronomy 27:9-10

When he [the king] is seated on his royal throne, he shall have a copy of this teaching written for him on a scroll by the levitical priests. Let it remain with him and let him read it all his life, so that he may learn to revere the Lord his God, to observe faithfully every word of this teaching as well as these laws.

> Deuteronomy 17:18-19

See, this day I set before you blessing and curse:
blessing, if you obey the commandments of the Lord
your God which I enjoin upon you this day; and curse,
if you do not obey the commandments of the Lord your
God, but turn away from the path which I enjoin upon
you this day and follow other gods, whom you have not
experienced.

Deuteronomy 11:26-28

This instruction which I enjoin upon you this day is not
too baffling for you, nor is it beyond reach. It is not in
the heavens, that you should say, 'Who among us can
go up to the heavens and get it for us and impart it to us,
that we may observe it?' Neither is it beyond the sea,
that you should say, 'Who among us can cross to the
other side of the sea and get it for us and impart it to us,
that we may observe it?' No, the thing is very close to
you, in your mouth and in your heart.

Deuteronomy 30:11-14

Other Gods

The first of the Ten Commandments revealed by God to Moses on Mount Sinai condemned idolatry: 'You shall have no other gods before Me ... you shall not make for yourself a graven image or any likeness of anything that is in the heavens above or on the earth below. You shall not bow down to them or serve them.' This central tenet of the faith has served as the foundation for all legislation concerning the worship of one God. According to Judaism, idolatry is one of the three cardinal sins (along with incest and murder) which must not be committed even if one's life has to be forfeited.

*

Hear, O Israel! The Lord is our God, the Lord alone.

Deuteronomy 6:4

You shall not make for yourselves a sculptured image, any likeness of what is in the heavens above, or on the earth below, or in the waters below the earth. You shall not bow down to them or serve them. For I the Lord your God am an impassioned God, visiting the guilt of the fathers upon the children, upon the third and upon the fourth generations of those who reject Me, but showing kindness to the thousandth generation of those who love Me and keep My commandments.

Deuteronomy 5:8

Know therefore this day and keep in mind that the Lord alone is God in heaven above and on earth below; there is no other.

Deuteronomy 4:39

You must destroy all the sites at which the nations you are to dispossess worshipped their gods, whether on lofty mountains and on hills or under any luxuriant tree. Tear down their altars, smash their pillars, put their sacred posts to the fire, and cut down the images of their gods, obliterating their name from that site.

Deuteronomy 12:2-3

When the Lord your God has cut down before you the nations which you are about to invade and dispossess, and you have dispossessed them and settled in their land, beware of being lured into their ways after they have been wiped out before you! Do not inquire about their gods, saying, 'How did those nations worship their gods? I too will follow those practices.'

Deuteronomy 12:29-30

If there appears among you a prophet or a dream-diviner and he gives you a sign or a portent, saying, 'Let us follow and worship another god' – whom you have not experienced – even if the sign or portent that he named to you comes true, do not heed the words of that prophet or that dream-diviner.

Deuteronomy 13:2-4

If your brother, your own mother's son, or your son or daughter, or the wife of your bosom, or your closest friend entices you in secret, saying, 'Come let us worship other gods' ... show him no pity or compassion, and do not shield him; but take his life.

Deuteronomy 13:7-10

When you enter the land that the Lord your God is giving you, you shall not learn to imitate the abhorrent practices of those nations. Let no one be found among you who consigns his son or daughter to the fire, or who is an augur, a soothsayer, a diviner, a sorcerer, one who casts spells, or one who consults ghosts or familiar spirits, or one who inquires of the dead.

Deuteronomy 18:9-11

Take care not to be lured away to serve other gods and bow to them. For the Lord's anger will flare up against you, and He will shut up the skies so that there will be no rain and the ground will not yield its produce; and you will soon perish from the good land that the Lord is giving you.

Deuteronomy 11:16-17

Well you know that we dwelt in the land of Egypt and that we passed through the midst of various other nations; and you have seen the detestable things and the fetishes of wood and stone, silver and gold, that they keep.

Deuteronomy 29:15-16

Perchance there is among you some man or woman, or some clan or tribe, whose heart is even now turning away from the Lord our God to go and worship the gods of those nations – perchance there is among you a stock sprouting poison weed and wormwood. When such a one hears the words of these sanctions, he may fancy himself immune, thinking 'I shall be safe, though I follow my own wilful heart' … the Lord will never forgive him; rather will the Lord's anger and passion rage against that man, till every sanction recorded in this book comes down upon him, and the Lord blots out his name from under heaven.

Deuteronomy 29:17-19

Do not turn to ghosts and do not inquire of familiar spirits.

Leviticus 19:31

You shall not practise divination or soothsaying.

Leviticus 19:26

You shall not tolerate a sorceress.

Exodus 22:17

Cursed be the man who makes a sculpture or molten image abhorred by the land, a craftsman's handiwork, and sets it up in secret.

Deuteronomy 27:15

If you hear it said, at one of the towns that the Lord your God is giving you to dwell in, that some scoundrels from among you have gone and subverted the inhabitants of their town, saying, 'Come let us worship other gods' – whom you have not experienced – you shall investigate and inquire and interrogate thoroughly. If it is true, the fact is established – that abhorrent thing was perpetrated in your midst – put the inhabitants of the town to the sword and put its cattle to the sword. Doom it and all that is in it to destruction.

Deuteronomy 13:13-16

You shall not act thus toward the Lord your God, for they perform for their gods every abhorrent act that the Lord detests; they even offer up their sons and daughters in fire to their gods.

Deuteronomy 12:31

Mark, the heavens to their uttermost reaches belong to the Lord your God, the earth and all that is on it!

Deuteronomy 10:14

Do not follow other gods, any gods of the people about you – for the Lord your God in your midst is an impassioned God – lest the anger of the Lord blaze forth against you and he wipe you off the face of the earth.

Deuteronomy 6:14-15

Only the Lord your God is God.

Deuteronomy 7:9

Justice

Many of the laws given on Mount Sinai deal with just action. According to the Jewish tradition, God's commandments to Israel are expressly for the purpose of establishing justice in the world. By acting in accordance with God's decrees, the Jewish people are able to bring about God's Kingdom on earth. Ultimately the entire range of ethical precepts is rooted in this concept.

*

Pick from each of your tribes men who are wise, discerning, and experienced, and I will appoint them as your heads.

Deuteronomy 1:13

Hear out your fellow men, and decide justly between any man and a fellow Israelite or stranger. You shall not be partial in judgment: hear out low and high alike. Fear no man, for judgment is God's.

Deuteronomy 1:16-17

You shall not subvert the rights of your needy in their disputes.

Exodus 23:6

You shall appoint magistrates and officials for your tribes, in all the settlements that the Lord your God is giving you, and they shall govern the people with due justice.

Deuteronomy 16:18

Nor must you show pity: life for life, eye for eye, tooth for tooth, hand for hand, foot for foot.

Deuteronomy 19:21

Do not take bribes, for bribes blind the clearsighted.

Exodus 23:8

You shall not render an unfair decision: do not favour the poor or show deference to the rich.

Leviticus 19:15

You shall not defraud your neighbour.

Leviticus 19:13

You shall not subvert the rights of your needy in their disputes.

Exodus 23:6

You must have completely honest weights and completely honest measures.

Deuteronomy 25:15

When there is a dispute between men and they go to law, and a decision is rendered acclaiming the one in the right, and the other in the wrong – if the guilty one is to be flogged, the magistrate shall have him lie down and be given lashes in his presence, by count, as his guilt warrants.

Deuteronomy 25:1-2

Parents shall not be put to death for children, nor children be put to death for parents: a person shall be put to death only for his own crime.

Deuteronomy 24:16

You must fulfil what has crossed your lips and perform what you have voluntarily vowed to the Lord your God, having made the promise with your own mouth.

Deuteronomy 23:24

When you make a vow to the Lord your God, do not put off fulfilling it.

Deuteronomy 23:22

If a man appears against another to testify maliciously and gives false testimony against him, the two parties to the dispute shall appear before the Lord, before the priests or magistrates in authority at the time, and the magistrates shall make a thorough investigation. If the man who testified is a false witness, if he has testified falsely against his fellow man, you shall do to him as he schemed to do to his fellow.

Deuteronomy 19:16-19

Cursed be he who subverts the rights of the stranger, the fatherless and the widow.

Deuteronomy 27:19

You shall not insult the deaf, or place a stumbling block before the blind.

Leviticus 19:14

You shall not judge unfairly: you shall show no partiality; you shall not take bribes, for bribes blind the eyes of the discerning and upset the plea of the just. Justice, justice shall you pursue.

Deuteronomy 16:18-20

Morality

The law revealed to Moses on Mount Sinai was concerned largely with moral behaviour. Among the various rules laid down by Moses were prescriptions regarding righteousness, self-restraint and deception. Not only are these commandments concerned with right action, but the inner world of thoughts, intentions and motives is of central importance. Moses addressed himself to the whole person in imploring the Hebrews to follow the divine law.

*

You shall not hate your kinsman in your heart.

Leviticus 19:17

You must not carry false rumours.

Exodus 23:1

You shall not swear falsely by the name of the Lord your God; for the Lord will not clear one who swears falsely by His name.

Deuteronomy 5:11

He who strikes his father or his mother shall be put to death.

Exodus 21:15

He who insults his father or his mother shall be put to death.

Exodus 21:16

You shall not ill-treat any widow or orphan.

Exodus 22:21

If a man has two wives, one loved and the other
unloved, and both the loved and the unloved have
borne him sons, but the first-born is the son of the
unloved one, when he wills his property to his sons, he
may not treat as first-born the son of the loved one in
disregard of the son of the unloved one who is older.

Deuteronomy 21:15-16

If a man has a wayward and defiant son, who does not
heed his father or mother and does not obey them even
after they discipline him, his father and mother shall
take hold of him and bring him out to the elders of his
town at the public place of his community. They shall
say to the elders of his town, 'This son of ours is disloyal
and defiant; he does not heed us. He is a glutton and a
drunkard.' Thereupon the men of his town shall stone
him to death.

Deuteronomy 21:18-20

If there is a needy person among you, one of your
kinsmen in any of your settlements in the land that the
Lord your God is giving you, do not harden your heart
and shut your hand against your needy kinsman.

Deuteronomy 15:7

If a fellow Hebrew, man or woman, is sold to you, he
shall serve you six years, and in the seventh year you
shall set him free.

Deuteronomy 15:12

If a man is guilty of a capital offence and is put to death,
and you impale him on a stake, you must not let his
corpse remain on the stake overnight, but must bury
him the same day.

Deuteronomy 21:22-23

When you see the ass of your enemy lying under its
burden and would refrain from raising it, you must
nevertheless raise it with him.

Exodus 23:5

If you see your fellow's ox or sheep gone astray, do not
ignore it; you must take it back to your fellow.

Deuteronomy 22:1

You shall not wrong a stranger or oppress him, for you were strangers in the land of Egypt.

Exodus 22:20

You shall not commit robbery.   Leviticus 19:13

You shall each revere his mother and his father.

Leviticus 19:3

He who fatally strikes a man shall be put to death.

Exodus 21:12

You shall not murder.   Deuteronomy 5:17

You shall rise before the aged and show deference to the old.

Leviticus 19:32

You shall not bear false witness against your neighbour.

Deuteronomy 5:17

You shall not steal.   Deuteronomy 5:17

You shall not covet your neighbour's wife. You shall not crave your neighbour's house, or his field, or his male or female slave, or his ox, or his ass, or anything that is your neighbour's.

Deuteronomy 5:18

Cursed be he who strikes down his neighbour in secret.

Deuteronomy 27:24

Cursed be he who misdirects a blind person on his way.

Deuteronomy 27:18

When you gather the grapes of your vineyard, do not pick it over again; that shall go to the stranger, the fatherless and the widow.

Deuteronomy 24:21

When you beat down the fruit of your olive trees, do not go over them again; that shall go to the stranger, the fatherless, and the widow.

Deuteronomy 24:20

When you reap the harvest in your field and overlook a sheaf in the field, do not turn back to get it; it shall go to the stranger, the fatherless and the widow.

Deuteronomy 24:19

You shall not abuse a needy and destitute stranger.

Deuteronomy 24:14

If a man is found to have kidnapped a fellow Israelite, enslaving him or selling him, that kidnapper shall die.

Deuteronomy 24:7

There will never cease to be needy ones in your land, which is why I command you: open your hand to the poor and needy kinsman in your land.

Deuteronomy 15:11

Men and Women

In delivering God's law to the Hebrews, Moses stressed the importance of sexual morality. According to Scripture, sex is an essential component of marriage. Woman was conceived because it is not good for man to be alone. The purpose of marriage is procreation as well as companionship. All sexual relations outside the matrimonial bond are forbidden, and Mosaic legislation condemns all illicit liaisons.

*

You shall not commit adultery.   Deuteronomy 5:17

Do not degrade your daughter and make her a harlot.
                                        Leviticus 19:29

A woman must not put on man's apparel, nor shall a man wear woman's clothing; for whoever does these things is abhorrent to the Lord your God.
                                        Deuteronomy 22:5

A man marries a woman and cohabits with her. Then he takes an aversion to her and makes up charges against her and defames her, saying, 'I married this woman; but when I approached her, I found that she was not a virgin.' In such a case the girl's father and mother shall produce the evidence of the girl's virginity before the elders of the town at the gate ... but if the charge proves true, the girl was found not to have been a virgin, then the girl shall be brought out to the entrance of her father's house, and the men of her town shall stone her to death.
                                        Deuteronomy 22:13-15, 20-21

If a man is found lying with another man's wife, both of them – the man and the woman with whom he lay – shall die.

Deuteronomy 22:22

In the case of a virgin who is engaged to a man – if a man comes upon her in town and lies with her, you shall take the two of them out to the gate of that town and stone them to death: the girl because she did not cry for help in the town, and the man because he violated his neighbour's wife.

Deuteronomy 22:23-24

No man shall marry his father's former wife.

Deuteronomy 23:1

No Israelite woman shall be a cult prostitute, nor shall any Israelite man be a cult prostitute.

Deuteronomy 23:18

Do not have carnal relations with any beast.

Leviticus 18:23

When you take the field against your enemies, and the Lord your God delivers them into your power and you take some of them captive, and you see among the natives a beautiful woman and you desire her and would take her to wife, you shall bring her into your house and she shall trim her hair, pare her nails, and discard her captive's garb. She shall spend a month's time in your house lamenting her father and mother; after that you may come to her and possess her, and she shall be your wife.

Deuteronomy 21:10-13

If two men get into a fight with each other, and the wife of one comes up to save her husband from his antagonist and puts out her hand and seizes him by his genitals, you shall cut off her hand: show no pity.

Deuteronomy 25:11-12

Cursed be he who lies with his mother-in-law.

Deuteronomy 27:23

Cursed be he who lies with his sister.

Deuteronomy 27:22

Cursed be he who lies with his father's wife.

Deuteronomy 27:20

When brothers dwell together and one of them dies and leaves no son ... her husband's brother shall unite with her: take her as his wife ... But if the man does not want to marry his brother's widow, his brother's widow shall appear before the elders in the gate and declare, 'My husband's brother refuses to establish a name in Israel for his brother.' The elders of his town shall then summon him and talk to him. If he insists saying, 'I do not want to marry her', his brother's widow shall go up to him in the presence of the elders, pull the sandal off his foot, spit in his face, and make this declaration. 'Thus shall be done to the man who will not build up his brother's house!'

Deuteronomy 25:5, 7-9

When a man has taken a bride, he shall not go out with the army or be assigned to it for any purpose; he shall be exempt one year for the sake of his household, to give happiness to the woman he has married.

Deuteronomy 24:5

If a man comes upon a virgin who is not engaged and he seizes her and lies with her, and they are discovered, the man who lay with her shall pay the girl's father fifty (shekels of) silver, and she shall be his wife. Because he has violated her, he can never have the right to divorce her.

Deuteronomy 22:28-29

Ritual

In addition to laws about moral behaviour, Moses charged the Hebrews to uphold ritual commandments. These prescriptions cover a wide range of practices including sacrifice, purity law, dietary regulations and festivals. By following these rules, the Jews are to become holy as God is holy.

*

You shall sanctify yourselves and be holy.

Leviticus 20:7

It is not with our fathers that the Lord made this covenant, but with us, the living, every one of us who is here today.

Deuteronomy 5:2

Observe the sabbath day and keep it holy, as the Lord your God has commanded you. Six days you shall labour and do all your work, but the seventh day is a sabbath of the Lord your God: you shall not do any work – you, your son or your daughter, your male or female slave, your ox or your ass, or any of your cattle, or the stranger in your settlements, so that your male and female slave may rest as you do. Remember that you were a slave in the land of Egypt and the Lord your God freed you from there, with a mighty hand and an outstretched arm; therefore the Lord your God has commanded you to observe the sabbath day.

Deuteronomy 5:12-15

You shall make tassels on the four corners of the garment with which you cover yourself.

Deuteronomy 22:12

Do not turn aside to the right or to the left: follow only
the path that the Lord your God has enjoined upon you.
Deuteronomy 5:29

No one whose testes are crushed or whose member is
cut off shall be admitted into the congregation of the
Lord.
Deuteronomy 23:2

You shall not eat anything abhorrent.
Deuteronomy 14:3

You shall not boil a kid in its mother's milk.
Deuteronomy 14:21

There shall be an area for you outside the camp where
you may relieve yourself. With your gear you shall have
a spike, and when you have squatted you shall dig a
hole with it and cover up your excrement.
Deuteronomy 23:13-14

This is what the Lord has commanded: Take from
among you gifts to the Lord, everyone whose heart so
moves him shall bring them – gifts for the Lord: gold,
silver, and copper; blue, purple, and crimson yarns, fine
linen, and goat's hair; tanned ram skins, dolphin skins,
and acacia wood oil for lighting, spices for the anointing
oil and for the aromatic incense, lapis lazuli and other
stones for setting, for the ephod and the breastpiece.
Exodus 35:4-9

On six days work may be done, but on the seventh day
you shall have a sabbath of complete rest, holy to the
Lord; whoever does any work on it shall be put to death.
Exodus: 35:2

When you enter the land that the Lord your God is
giving you as a heritage, and you occupy it and settle in
it, you shall take some of the first fruit of the soil, which
you harvest from the land that the Lord your God is
giving you, put it in a basket and go to the place where
the Lord your God will choose to establish his name.
Deuteronomy 26:1-2

If, along the road, you chance upon a bird's nest, in any tree or on the ground, with fledglings or eggs and the mother sitting over the fledglings or on the eggs, do not take the mother together with her young. Let the mother go, and take only the young.

Deuteronomy 22:7

When the Lord your God has cut down the nations whose land the Lord your God is giving you, and you have dispossessed them and settled in their towns and homes, you shall set aside three cities in the land that the Lord your God is giving you to possess ... so that any manslayer may have a place to flee to.

Deuteronomy 19:1-3

You shall not sacrifice to the Lord your God an ox or a sheep that has any defect of a serious kind, for that is abhorrent to the Lord your God.

Deuteronomy 17:1

Three times a year – on the Feast of Unleavened Bread, on the Festival of Weeks, and on the Feast of Broths – all your males shall appear before the Lord your God in the place that He will choose. They shall not appear before the Lord emptyhanded, but each with his own gift, according to the blessing that the Lord your God has bestowed upon you.

Deuteronomy 16:16-17

You shall slaughter the passover sacrifice for the Lord your God, from the flock and the herd, in the place where the Lord will choose to establish His name. You shall not eat anything leavened with it; for seven days thereafter you shall eat unleavened bread, bread of distress – for you departed from the land of Egypt hurriedly – so that you may remember the day of your departure from the Land of Egypt as long as you live.

Deuteronomy 16:2-3

You may eat any clean bird. The following you may not eat: the eagle, the vulture, the kite, the falcon, and the buzzard of any variety; every variety of raven; the ostrich, the nighthawk, the sea gull, and the hawk of any variety; the little owl, the great owl, and the white owl; the pelican, the bustard, and the cormorant; the stork, any variety of heron, the hoopoe, and the bat.

Deuteronomy 14:11-18

All winged swarming things are unclean for you: they may not be eaten.   Deuteronomy 14:19

These you may eat of all that live in the water: you may eat anything that has fins and scales. But you may not eat anything that has no fins and scales: it is unclean for you.   Deuteronomy 14:9-10

You shall not eat anything abhorrent. These are the animals that you may eat: the ox, the sheep and the goat, the ibex, the antelope, the mountain sheep, and any other animal that has true hoofs which are cleft in two and brings up the cud – such you may eat.

Deuteronomy 14:3-6

You shall not gash yourselves or shave the front of your heads because of the dead.   Deuteronomy 14:1

Make sure that you do not partake of the blood; for the blood is the life.   Deuteronomy 12:23

Observe them faithfully, for that will be proof of your wisdom and discernment to other peoples who on hearing of all these laws will say, 'Surely, that great nation is a wise and discerning people.' For what great nation is there that has a god so close at hand as is the Lord our God whenever we call upon Him?

Deuteronomy 4:6-7

Cut away, therefore, the thickening about your hearts and stiffen your necks no more.   Deuteronomy 10:16

The Promised Land

According to Scripture, God decreed that the Hebrews would eventually inherit the Promised Land – the territory promised to Abraham for his descendants. Repeatedly Moses told the people that this would be their inheritance. Yet he himself was not allowed to enter it because he had disobeyed God's command. When he went up to Mount Nebo to die, God showed him the entire country which the Hebrew nation would possess.

*

Go, take possession of the land that the Lord swore to your fathers, Abraham, Isaac, and Jacob, to give to them and to their offspring after them.

Deuteronomy 1:8

I will send forth My terror before you, and I will throw into panic all the people among whom you come, and I will make your enemies turn tail before you.

Exodus 23:27

Yet you refused to go up, and flouted the command of the Lord your God. You sulked in your tents and said, 'It is because the Lord hates us that He brought us out of the land of Egypt to hand us over to the Amorites to wipe us out. What kind of place are we going to?'

Deuteronomy 1:26-28

When you take the field against your enemies, and see horses and chariots – forces larger than yours – have no fear of them, for the Lord your God, who brought you from the land of Egypt, is with you.

Deuteronomy 20:1

Before you join battle, the priest shall come forward, and address the troops. He shall say to them, 'Hear, O Israel! You are about to join battle with our enemy. Let not your courage falter. Do not be in fear, or in panic, or in dread of them. For it is the Lord your God who marches with you to do battle for you against your enemy, to bring you victory.'

Deuteronomy 20:2-4

The Lord your God has given you this country to possess. You must go as shock-troops, warriors all, at the head of your Israelite kinsmen. Only your wives, children, and livestock ... shall be left in the towns I have assigned to you, until the Lord has granted your kinsmen a haven such as you have, and they too have taken possession of the land that the Lord your God is giving them, beyond the Jordan.

Deuteronomy 3:18-20

I spoke to you, but you would not listen; you flouted the Lord's command and wilfully marched into the hill country. Then the Amorites who lived in those hills came out against you like so many bees and chased you.

Deuteronomy 1:43-44

When you approach a town to attack it, you shall offer it terms of peace.

Deuteronomy 20:10

When in your war against a city you have to besiege it a long time in order to capture it, you must not destroy its trees, wielding the axe against them. You may eat of them, but you must not cut them down. Are trees of the field human to withdraw before you into the besieged city?

Deuteronomy 20:19

When the Lord your God brings you to the land that you are about to invade and occupy, and He dislodges many nations before you ... and the Lord your God delivers them to you and you defeat them, you must doom them to destruction: grant them no terms and give them no quarter.

Deuteronomy 7:1-2

All the peoples of the earth shall see that the Lord's name is proclaimed over you, and they shall stand in fear of you.

Deuteronomy 28:10

You will dominate many nations, but they will not dominate you.

Deuteronomy 15:6

There shall be no needy among you – since the Lord your God will bless you in the land which the Lord your God is giving you as a hereditary portion.

Deuteronomy 15:4

Every spot on which your foot treads shall be yours: your territory shall extend from the wilderness to the Lebanon and from the river – the Euphrates – to the western sea.

Deuteronomy 11:24

The land which you are about to invade and occupy is not like a vegetable garden; but the land you are about to cross into and occupy, a land of hills and valleys, soaks up its water from the rains of heaven.

Deuteronomy 11:10-11

When the Lord your God has thrust them from your path, say not to yourselves, 'The Lord has enabled me to occupy this land because of my virtues', it is rather because of the wickedness of those nations that the Lord is dispossessing them before you.

Deuteronomy 9:4

For the Lord your God is bringing you into a good land, a land with streams and springs and fountains issuing from plain and hill; a land of wheat and barley, of wines, figs, and pomegranates, a land of olive trees and honey, a land where you may eat food without stint, where you lack nothing; a land whose rocks are iron and from whose hills you can mine copper.

Deuteronomy 8:7-9

The Lord your God will deliver them up to you,
throwing them into utter panic until they are wiped out.
He will deliver their kings into your hand, and you shall
obliterate their name from under the heavens; no man
shall stand up to you, until you have wiped them out.

Deuteronomy 7:23-24

Should you say to yourselves, 'These nations are more
numerous than we; how can we dispossess them?' You
need have no fear of them. You have but to bear in mind
what the Lord your God did to Pharaoh and all the
Egyptians.

Deuteronomy 7:17-18

You shall destroy all the peoples that the Lord your God
delivers to you, showing them no pity.

Deuteronomy 7:16

If, after you have entered the land that the Lord your
God has given you, and occupied it and settled in it, you
decide, 'I will set a king over me, as do all the nations
about me', you shall be free to set a king over yourself,
one chosen by the Lord your God.

Deuteronomy 17:14-15

When the Lord your God brings you into the land which
He swore to your fathers, Abraham, Isaac and Jacob, to
give you – great and flourishing cities which you did not
build, houses full of good things which you did not fill,
hewn cisterns which you did not hew, vineyards and
olive groves which you did not plant – and you eat your
fill, take heed that you do not forget the Lord who freed
you from the land of Egypt, the house of bondage.

Deuteronomy 6:10-12

O Lord, God, You who let Your servant see the first
works of Your greatness and Your mighty hand, You
whose powerful deeds no god in heaven or on earth can
equal. Let me, I pray, cross over and see the good land
on the other side of the Jordan.

Deuteronomy 3:23-25

Blessed shall you be in the city and blessed shall you be in the country.

Deuteronomy 28:3

When the Lord heard your loud complaint, He was angry. He vowed: Not one of these men, this evil generation, shall see the good land that I swore to give to your fathers ... Because of you the Lord was incensed with me too, and He said: 'You shall not enter it either.'

Deuteronomy 1:34-35,37

Your little ones whom you said would be carried off, your children who do not yet know good from bad, they shall enter it; to them will I give it and they shall possess it.

Deuteronomy 1:39

Turn from Your blazing anger, and renounce the plan to punish Your people. Remember Your servants, Abraham, Isaac, and Jacob, how You swore to them by Your Self and said to them: I will make your offspring as numerous as the stars of heaven, and I will give to your offspring this whole land of which I spoke, to possess forever.

Exodus 32:12-13

Obey, O Israel, willingly and faithfully, that it may go well with you and that you may increase greatly in a land flowing with milk and honey.

Deuteronomy 6:3

Should you, when you have begotten children and children's children and are long established in the land, act wickedly and make for yourselves a sculptured image in any likeness, causing the Lord your God displeasure and vexation, I call heaven and earth this day to witness against you that you shall soon perish from the land which you are crossing the Jordan to occupy; you shall not long endure in it, but shall be utterly wiped out. The Lord will scatter you among the peoples, and only a scant few of you shall be left among the nations to which the Lord will drive you. There you will serve man-made gods of wood and stone, that cannot see or hear or eat or smell.

Deuteronomy 4:25-28

The Lord will bring a nation against you from afar, from the end of the earth, which will swoop down like the eagle – a nation whose language you do not understand, a ruthless nation, that will show the old no regard and the young no mercy.

Deuteronomy 28:49-50

The Lord was angry with me on your account and swore that I should not cross the Jordan and enter the good land that the Lord your God is giving you as a heritage. For I must die in this land; I shall not cross the Jordan. But you will cross and take possession of that good land.

Deuteronomy 4: 21-22

The Lord bless you and keep you! The Lord deal kindly and graciously with you! The Lord bestow His favour upon you and grant you peace!

Numbers 6:24-26

Blessed shall you be in your comings and blessed shall you be in your goings.

Deuteronomy 28:6

May the Lord, the God of your fathers, increase your numbers a thousandfold, and bless you as He promised you.

Deuteronomy 1:11

I am now one hundred and twenty years old, I can no longer be active. Moreover, the Lord has said to me, 'You shall not go across yonder Jordan.' The Lord your

God Himself will cross over at your head; and He will
wipe out those nations from your path and you shall
dispossess them – Joshua is the one who shall cross at
your head.

Deuteronomy 31:2-3

It is not because you are the most numerous of peoples
that the Lord set His heart upon you and chose you –
indeed, you are the smallest of peoples; but it was
because the Lord loved you.

Deuteronomy 7:7-8

Give ear, O heavens, let me speak; Let the earth hear the
words I utter! May my discourse come down as the rain,
my speech distill as the dew, like showers on young
growth, like droplets on the grass. For the name of the
Lord I proclaim; Give glory to our God!

Deuteronomy 32:1-3

Moses through the Rabbis

The words of Moses are recorded in Genesis, Exodus, Leviticus, Numbers and Deuteronomy, while in rabbinic literature the rabbis speculated about Moses' life and teaching. In commentaries on Scripture, they formulated interpretations of the meaning of Moses' sayings and the significance of his message. Their writings provide a vision of Moses different in many ways from what is found in the Five Books. Although these rabbinic sources are not authoritative, they have profoundly influenced the development of Jewish thought through the ages. (The rabbinic sources for the passages in this section are given in the standard abbreviations.)

*

Moses began to argue about God's decisions, and to contend with God, and to criticise His ways.... Therefore the Attribute of Justice sought to punish Moses, but when God reflected that it was because of Israel's distress that Moses spoke thus, God dealt with him according to His Attribute of Mercy. The Rabbis also point out that Abraham, Isaac and Jacob, in spite of many trials, did not 'criticise God's ways'; they did not do so, even though God did not reveal Himself to them by His true name of Yahweh, the Merciful One, as He revealed Himself to Moses. They did not even ask God what His name was, as Moses had asked him (Exodus 3:13). And, later, when God said that He had hearkened to the groaning of the children of Israel, this was because they had not criticised Him.

Exod.R., Wa'era, VI, 1–4

God said to Moses: 'Write thee these things, for it is by means of these things that I have made a covenant with Israel' (Exodus 34:27). When God was about to give the

Torah, He recited it to Moses in due order, Scriptures, Mishnah, Agada, and Talmud, for God spake *all* these words (20:1), even the answers to questions which distinguished scholars in the future are destined to ask their teachers did God reveal to Moses, for He spake *all* these things. Then, when God had ended, He said to Moses 'Go and teach it to my sons'.... Moses said, 'Lord, do thou write it for them.' God said, 'I did indeed desire to give it all to them in writing, but it was revealed that the Gentiles in the future will have dominion over them, and will claim the Torah as theirs; then would my children be like the Gentiles. Therefore give them the Scriptures in writing, and Mishnah, Agada and Talmud orally, for it is they which separate Israel and the Gentiles.'   *Tanḥ.B.*, Ki Tissa, 58*b*

When Moses came down from God, Satan came before God and said, 'Where is the Torah?' God said, 'I have given it to the earth.' Satan went to the earth and said, 'Where is the Torah?' The earth replied, 'God [alone] knows the way thereof' (Job 28:23). Then he went to the sea and to the deep, and they said, 'It is not with us' (Job 28:14). Then he returned and said to God, 'I have enquired all over the earth, and have not found it.' God said, 'Go to the son of Amram.' So he went to Moses, and said to him, 'Where is the Law which God gave to you?' Moses said, 'What am I that God should have given the Torah to me?' Then God said, 'Moses, are you a liar?' Then Moses said, 'This lovely and hidden thing in which day by day thou tookest thy pleasure, should *I* take the credit of it?' ... Then God said, 'Because you have made yourself small, therefore it shall be called by thy name,' as it says, 'Remember the Law of Moses, my servant' (Malachi 3:2).   *Sab.* 89*a*

R. Joshua b. Levi said: When Moses went up to God, the angels said, 'What has a son of woman to do among us?' God said, 'He has come to receive the Law.' Then they said, 'The beautiful Torah, which thou hast hidden away since creation and for 974 generations before creation, dost thou purpose to give it to one of flesh and blood?' Then God said, 'Moses, answer them!' Moses replied, 'I fear they may burn me with the breath of their

mouths.' God said, 'Hold fast to my throne of glory, and
answer them....' Then Moses said, 'What is written in
the Law which thou gavest me, "I am the Lord your
God who brought you forth from Egypt," Did you' – he
said to the angels – 'go down to Egypt? Were you
enslaved by Pharaoh? What need have you of the Law?
It is written, "Ye shall have no other gods." Do you
dwell among the uncircumcised who practise idolatry?
It says, "Remember the Sabbath day." Do you do any
work, so that you need a day of rest? … It says, "Honour
thy father and mother." Have you any fathers and
mothers? It says, "Do no murder, do not steal or commit
adultery"; is there any envy, is there any Evil Inclination
among you?' Then they praised God, and became the
friends of Moses.   *Sab.* 88b–89a

R. Judah said in the name of Rab: When Moses went up
to God, he found God sitting and putting little crowns
on the top of the letters of the Law. He said to God,
'Who is it that forces thee to put crowns to the letters of
the Law' [which thou hast already written]? He replied,
'A man is to appear on earth after many generations,
Akiba b. Joseph by name, who will expound for each tip
of every letter of the Law heaps and heaps of rulings'
[*Halakot*]. Then Moses said, 'Show him to me.' God
replied, 'Turn round.' So he did, and he went and sat at
the end of the eighth row [of students listening to R.
Akiba], and he did not understand anything of what
was being said, and his strength abated. When Akiba
came to a certain matter [which needed proof], and his
disciples asked him how he knew this, Akiba replied,
'This is a teaching which was delivered to Moses on
Sinai.' Then the mind of Moses was quieted. Then he
went back to God, and said, 'Thou hast a man like this,
and thou givest the Torah through *me*?' Then God said,
'Be silent; thus it has seemed good to me.' Then Moses
said, 'Thou hast shown me his knowledge of the Torah;
show me now his reward.' Then God said, 'Turn round.'
He did so, and he saw the flesh of Akiba being weighed
in the meat market. Then he said, 'Such is his
knowledge of the Law, and such is his reward?' Then
God said, 'Silence, so it has seemed good to me.'
                                                    Men. 29b

'And it came to pass when Moses held up his hand that Israel prevailed, and when he let down his hand, Amalek prevailed' (Exodus 17:11). But could the hands of Moses promote the battle or hinder the battle? – it is, rather, to teach you that such time as the Israelites directed their thoughts on high, and kept their hearts in subjection to their Father in heaven, they prevailed; otherwise they suffered defeat. After the like manner it says, 'Make thee a fiery serpent, and set it upon a standard, and it shall come to pass that if a man is bitten, when he sees it, he shall live' (Numbers 21:8). But could the serpent slay, or the serpent keep alive? – it is, rather, to teach you that such time as the Israelites directed their thoughts on high, and kept their hearts in subjection to their Father in heaven, they were healed; otherwise they pined away.   *R.H. III, 8*

It is written in Exodus 17:2 that the people murmured against Moses, and Moses cried unto God, 'They are almost ready to stone me.' Moses said to God, 'Make known to me if they are going to kill me.' God said to him, 'What is that to thee? Pass over before the people' (Exodus 17:5). R. Me'ir said: These words mean, 'Be like unto me. As I return good for evil, so do thou return good for evil,' as it is said, 'Who is a God like thee, forgiving sin, and *passing over* transgression' (Micah 7:18).   *Exod.R, Beshallaḥ, XXVI, 2*

It says in Numbers 20:12, 'Because he believed not in me', after the striking of the rock. Hence Moses was not allowed to enter the land. But did Moses never show a greater lack of faith? Did he not say, 'If flocks and herds were slaughtered for them, it would not suffice?' (Numbers 11:22). Why did not God pass sentence on him *then*? It is like a king who had a friend who behaved overbearingly to him in private, but the king paid no attention to him. Some days afterwards, he acted similarly to him in the presence of the legions. Then the king sentenced him to death. So God said to Moses, 'I took no account of thy first action because it was in private; but now I cannot overlook it, because this sin was before the multitude,' as it says, 'In that ye did not sanctify me in the sight of the children of Israel' (Numbers 20:12).   *Tanḥ.B., Ḥuḳḳat, 61a*

'And this is the blessing which Moses ...' (Deuteronomy 33: 1). Moses did not begin with Israel's needs, until he had opened with God's praise. He was like an orator, standing by the judge's seat, who was hired by a client to plead for him. But before speaking of the client's needs, the orator opened with the praises of the king, saying, 'Happy is the world by reason of his rule, by reason of his justice': all the people joined in the praise. Then he opened his client's case; he ended, too, with praise of the king. So did Moses. So, too, did David and Solomon. So, too, did the Elders who composed the Eighteen Benedictions for Israel to use in prayer. They did not open with Israel's needs, but with, 'The great, mighty, and awful God,' 'Holy art thou and awful is thy name.' Only then came, 'Thou loosest the bound and healest the sick.' Finally they ended with, 'We give thee thanks.'

Sifre Deut., Berakah, §343, f. 142*a, b*

God said to Moses, 'I will send thee to Pharaoh.' Moses answered, 'Lord of the world, I cannot; for Jethro has received me, and opened his house door to me, so that I am as a son with him. If a man opens his house to his fellow, his guest owes his life to him. Jethro has received me, and has honourably entertained me; can I depart without his leave?' Hence it says, 'Moses went and returned to Jethro his father-in-law' (Exodus 4:18).

Tanḥ., Shemot, § 16, f. 87*a*

And the people came to Moses and said, 'We have sinned, for we have spoken against the Lord, and against thee' (Numbers 21:7). At once Moses prayed for them. This shows you the humility of Moses in that he did not delay to seek mercy for them, and it shows further the power of repentance. As soon as they said, 'We have sinned,' instantly he was reconciled to them. For one who pardons can never become cruel. And how do you know that if a man asks pardon of his neighbour whom he has offended, and that if the neighbour refuses to pardon him, he, the neighbour, and not the offender, is called a sinner? Because Samuel said, 'As for

me, far be it from me to sin unto the Lord by refraining
to pray for you' (I Samuel 12:23). When was this? When
the people came and said, 'We have sinned.'

Tanḥ.B., Ḥuḳḳat, 63b

God told Moses to make war on Sihon (Deuteronomy
2:24), but Israel did not make war: they sent messengers
of peace (*ib*: 26). God said, 'I ordered you to make war,
but you made overtures for peace.' 'There is no peace,
says the Lord, for the wicked' (Isaiah 48:22). How great,
then, must be words of peace, if Israel disobeyed God
for peace's sake, and yet He was not wrath with them.

Tanḥ.B., Debarim, 3b

When Moses came down from Mount Sinai, and saw
how corrupt Israel had become, he gazed at the Tablets,
and saw that the letters which were on them had flown
away from the stone. So he broke the Tablets beneath
the mountain. Immediately he became dumb, and was
unable to utter a word. At that very time a decree was
issued concerning Israel that Israel should learn them
[i.e. the commandments] through affliction and
enslavement, through exile and banishment, through
straits and through famine. And on account of that
suffering which they have undergone, God will repay
their recompense in the days of the Messiah many times
over.

Tan.d.b.El. p. 117

'And Moses sent his father-in-law away' (Exodus 18:27).
R. Elazar of Modi'im said: That is, he gave him many
gifts, as we may learn from what Moses said to him,
'Leave us not, I pray thee' (Numbers 10:31). He said to
him, 'You gave us good counsel, and God approved of
it; do not leave us.' But Moses' father-in-law said to
Moses, 'Is the lamp of any value except in a place of
darkness? Is the lamp of value between the sun and the
moon? You are the sun, and Aaron, your brother, is the
moon; what can the lamp do between you two? I will go
to mine own land, and I will convert all the children of
my country, and I will bring them to the Law, and I will
draw them near under the wings of the Shechinah.'

Mek., Amalek, Yitro, §2, p. 199 *fin.*; *Mek.*, §4, vol. II, p. 185

When Moses heard his doom, he urged every argument to secure a remission of his sentence. Amongst other things he said, 'Sovereign of the universe, arise from the judgment seat, and sit on the throne of mercy, so that I die not. Let my sins be forgiven by reason of bodily sufferings which may come upon me. But put me not in the power of the angel of death. If thou wilt do this, then will I proclaim thy praise before all the inhabitants of the world, as David said, I shall not die, but live, and declare the works of the Lord' (Psalm 118:17). Then God said to Moses, 'Hear the rest of the verse, "This is the gate of the Lord, through which the righteous shall enter." ' For all creatures death has been prepared from the beginning.   *Tanḥ.B., Wa'etḥanan, 6a*

R. Me'ir said: Whence is the Resurrection derived from the Torah? As it is said, 'Then will Moses and the children of Israel sing this song unto the Lord' (Exodus 15:1). It is not said 'sang', but 'will sing'; hence the Resurrection is deducible from the Torah. Again, R. Joshua b. Levi asked: Whence is the Resurrection derived from the Torah? As it is said, 'Blessed are they that dwell in thy house, they will be still praising thee' (Psalm 84:4). It is not stated, 'They will have praised thee', but 'will be still praising thee' [in the Hereafter]; hence the Resurrection is deducible from the Torah.
                    San. 91b

Moses said to God, 'When I come to the children of Israel and they ask me who sent me, what shall I say?' For Moses wished to ask God to reveal His great name to him. God replied, 'Moses, is it my name that thou seekest to know? According to my acts am I called. When I judge my creatures, I am called Elohim or Judge (Exodus 22:27); when I punish my enemies, Lord of Hosts; when I suspend judgement over man's sin, El Shaddai (Almighty God); when I sit with the attribute of mercy, I am called the Compassionate One. According as my acts are, so is my name.'
                    Tanḥ., Shemot, §20, f. 88b

When God said, 'Make me a dwelling place,' Moses wondered, and said, 'The glory of God fills the upper and the lower worlds, and yet He says to me, Make me a dwelling place....' God said, 'Not as thou deemest so do I deem, but twenty boards to the north, and twenty to the south, and eight to the west (are enough for me) (Exodus 26:18, 20, 25). And not only that, but I will come down and confine my Shechinah within a square yard.... Ye are the children of the Lord your God, and I am your Father (Deuteronomy 14:1; Jeremiah 31:9). It is an honour to children to be near their father, and an honour to a father to be near his children; therefore, make a house for the Father that He may dwell near His children.'

Exod.R., Terumah, XXXIV, 1, 3

While Moses was feeding the sheep of his father-in-law in the wilderness, a young kid ran away. Moses followed it until it reached a ravine, where it found a well to drink from. When Moses reached it, he said, 'I did not know that you ran away because you were thirsty. Now you must be weary.' He carried the kid back. Then God said, 'Because thou hast shown pity in leading back one of a flock belonging to a man, thou shalt lead *my* flock, Israel.'

Exod.R., Shemot, II, 2